# Rescued From Darkness

*Helping Others Find Deliverance in Christ*

By

Luciano Pereira da Silva

eBook ISBN: 978-1-965161-65-4

Paperback ISBN: 978-1-965161-66-1

Hardback ISBN: 978-1-965161-67-8

# Contents

# Dedication

First of all, to Jesus–the Master Deliverer, who reconciled me with God and gave me the ministry of reconciliation.

To my beloved and dear wife, Shirley, who has been a companion in everything, including in the ministry of deliverance.

To my dear little daughter, Maria Fernanda--missionary, full of the Holy Spirit, adorer, truly special girl who has taught us so much.

# Foreword

**"These 12 Jesus sent out with the following instructions: "Do not go among the Gentiles or enter any town of the Samaritans. Go rather to the lost sheep of Israel. As you go, proclaim this message: 'The kingdom of heaven has come near.' Heal the sick, raise the dead, cleanse those who have leprosy, and drive out demons. Freely you have received; freely give." (Matthew 10:5-8, NIV)**

In the very early 1990s, I recall vividly joining thousands of other believers who were singing along passionately with Christian musician Carman, "For I know there's a God in heaven, who saves, delivers, and heals…" It is a beautiful song, and that evening, it was clear that most of those present believed every word that Carman was singing. But as those lyrics washed over me, I vividly recall being struck by two thoughts in that moment.

First, we really do have a Lord who does all three things: saves, delivers, and heals.

Second, while the Church still seems to embrace the idea of the Lord as savior, and even as healer, we somewhere seem to have lost our confidence in Him as a deliverer.

At that stage of my life, I had already been in church for years and was serving as a pastor. Yet it occurred to me that I could count on one hand the number of times I had even heard the idea of deliverance mentioned in church. I began to consider that something might be missing from the church and from my ministry, something important.

The lack of awareness of deliverance in so many churches, and its absence in the ministry of most disciples, is all the sadder because of how explicit our Lord Jesus was in indicating its importance. From the beginning, as we see in Matthew, chapter 10, Jesus made it clear not only that His disciples were sent out to do ministry but also exactly what that ministry involved.

Those initial disciples, and all subsequent ones, were called to proclaim the kingdom of heaven (so that people might be saved), to heal the sick (because we serve a Lord Who heals), And to drive out demons (to deliver people). This command to drive out demons and the authority given by Jesus to His disciples to do so is a common feature in nearly every sending forth that Jesus did. And there is nothing in scripture, nor anywhere else, to suggest that this important part of the calling was ever intended to end. So, what has happened?

In my observation, many in the church are ignorant of the reality of evil forces in our world, or they explain them away with modern psychological language or with alternate explanations. Others, while aware of the presence of Satan and demonic oppression, have developed an unbiblical and irrational fear of engaging with this part of our reality.

Likewise, there are some who not only realize that these realities exist but also understand that in the name of Jesus, disciples are still called to engage in the ministry of deliverance, yet they believe that this is a ministry set apart for a special class of super-spiritual believers with some special powers. And then, of course, there are some who simply don't want to be obedient in this part of the call to discipleship. Rather than get into the ugly reality of people's challenges and bondage to see them become free, these comfortable believers would rather look away and pretend not to notice those bound up and in need of deliverance. It is too uncomfortable otherwise.

For all these reasons, I am pleased that you have found your way to this short, simple, and applicable book. My dear friend and ministry colleague, the Reverend Luciano Pereira da Silva, has opened his heart with humility, authenticity, and insight to share one person's personal journey into deliverance, both in his own life and as a powerful part of his ministry.

With personal stories from his decades of ministry experience, powerful anecdotes of both successes and setbacks and setting it all in the context of scripture, Luciano has given us a primer on not only overcoming our objections to deliverance ministry but also moving into it in practical and spiritually sound ways. Do you find yourself fearful in the face of this sort of ministry calling? Fear not!

There is a way forward. Do you sense that you need some special powers or giftings for this sort of ministry? Read on. You will discover that the power belongs to the Lord and the authority for this ministry is willingly given by Him for all of us who will be obedient to the calling. Unsure of how to proceed or what to do? Rather than giving specific answers, Luciano will point you to the Source of those answers, the One who is able to bring to us an understanding of all things. And in the end, you will be encouraged, inspired, and awed by the power of our amazing Lord simply by reading these wonderful stories of deliverance, all because of a humble servant who has been willing to trust the Lord and step into the moments (and his fears and uncertainties) for the sake of others, and for the glory of God.

One of my favorite stories from the life of Martin Luther, the leader of the Protestant Reformation, may be apocryphal. I don't think we can know for sure. But if it didn't happen, it should have because it conveys an important truth. It is said that when Luther was an Augustinian monk, he was in his cell praying late one evening when he became sleepy. Putting out his lamp, he turned over to his bed to sleep when, in his telling, he became aware of something powerful and evil present in the cell with him.

Relighting his lamp, Luther says that he came face to face with the personification of Satan himself, hovering over him in his bed. Upon realizing who and what it was, Luther reportedly said, "Oh, it's only you!" He blew out the lamp and rolled over to sleep, whereupon the presence of evil fled his cell.

I love that story. Luther was in no way attempting to lessen the danger of Satan nor to minimize the risk of evil in our lives and in our world. He was simply assured that the light, the fire, the power that dwelt within him was so much more powerful than the one who had come to frighten him that he need not be afraid. There are only two ways that evil gets the upper hand in the lives of Christians. Either we open doors of invitation in our lives, knowingly or unknowingly, and invite the demonic in (an invitation they will always accept). Or do we overlook or deny the power of the Lord and His disciples to deliver us from that evil once it is present in our lives? The solution to both issues is simple. Let's recover an understanding of deliverance ministry in the life of all disciples and embrace its practice in our churches, in our homes, and in our communities. Unsure how to do that? Pastor Luciano's book is a good place to start because, at the end of the day, Carman is not the only one who knows there's a God in heaven who saves, delivers, and heals.

**The Rev. Max Wilkins retired in May 2024 after 42 years of ministry, including 10 years as president and CEO of TMS Global, where he served from 2014-2024. He presently serves the Commission on Evangelism, Mission and Church Planting for the Global Methodist Church.**

Pastor Luciano has written a book that will bring hope to those who are oppressed by the demonic and to those who love them.

Some dismiss the reality of Satan or the demonic. But Jesus not only knew the reality of the devil, but He also came to destroy the works of the devil (1 John 3:8). One of the ways he did this was to cast demons from people and teach his followers to do the same.

*When Jesus had called the Twelve together, he gave them power and authority to drive out all demons and to cure diseases (Luke 9:1).*

Some people will not experience the freedom of God until they are set free from the demonic. We don't serve people well if we do not use the power God gives us to free people from the enemy when they are bound.

I have known Pastor Luciano and seen the fruit of his ministry. God has brought many people into the family of God through him and helped them find release from the oppression of the enemy.

He is a mature man of God with a deep compassion for people and an unshakeable commitment to Jesus and his purposes.

This is a book that brings hope. In these pages, you will learn that the works of the devil in afflicted persons can be destroyed by the power of God.

*--The Rev. Dr. Steve Cordle is the executive director of The River Network International in Pittsburgh, Pennsylvania, USA*

# Introduction

Deliverance of people who are tormented by demons has been a frequent part of my ministry. Therefore, I was prompted by the Holy Spirit to share what God has placed on my heart and accomplished in my life. I do not intend to exhaust the subject, which certainly is vast, but I will try to bring light on the subject through my experience and knowledge of the Word. Truthfully, I never imagined that I would ever work in this kind of ministry.

I still remember the first time I saw a demonic manifestation. Early in my life with God, I went to a prayer night in a Church of friends in the city the name Jacarezinho. While there, a woman was thrown to the ground and rolled back and forth. I do not remember what happened after that. I was shocked to see such blatant demonic activity. Little did I realize that one day, I would be used by God in the ministry of deliverance.

In this book I will report real cases that I witnessed and give some practical guidance for ministering deliverance to others. When the Spirit of God reveals demonic activity, the first step may be to pray and cast them out in the name of Jesus. But that is not the end. We also need to help the person become completely free and spiritually whole. I will try to provide a simple guide to understanding deliverance.

This book is not only about theory and head knowledge; it is about the application. What I describe here comes from my practice of day-to-day ministry, attending to many people and praying with them in diverse places. I hope that you may grow in faith and develop in your ministry. And most of all, I pray that you will be free!

"Behold, I have given you authority to tread on serpents and scorpions and over all the power of the enemy, and nothing will harm you" **(Luke 10:19).**

# Chapter 1
# Christ Delivered and Called Me

*"For I received from the Lord what I also passed on to you..."*

*1 Corinthians 11:23*

In *1 Corinthians 11*, the Apostle Paul told the Church that he was passing on what he had received from the Lord regarding Communion. Similarly, when it comes to the ministry of deliverance, I am passing on what I experienced. Most of the time, the Lord touches us and then we can share our experience with others. He works in our own lives first. Through my conversion experience, I had to be delivered from the presence of evil spirits within me.

I grew up in Brazil with two brothers. The oldest was Wellington. My middle brother was Marcelo. And I was the youngest. Marcelo was born with mental problems. My mother took him to many doctors. However, due to a lack of medical information at that time, we never received any answers. He died when he was seven years old.

When I was growing up, my family was troubled. My father often came home, beat my mother, and broke things. This was a strong indicator of a spiritual problem.

One time, when I was young, I had a plastic toy that was probably a gift from my mother. My toy was sitting on a dresser in my bedroom when my father came home drunk. He broke things around the house and destroyed my little toy with his bare hands. I was very sad because I did not have many toys. That experience marked me.

Today, I realized that there was a spirit of violence inside my house. For example, one day, my father kicked my mom in the back, and she fell down the stairs. I was there at the foot of the stairs, witnessing it all.

Another time, my father was having an adulterous affair. The woman came to our home during the early morning hours and created a scandal. I saw my mother's humiliation, and I, too, felt ashamed.

These sinful attitudes and actions were manifestations of demons at work in my parents and in the life of my family. Exposure to these traumas gave demons permission to disturb me and bind me. That was my reality for a long time.

Once I was 30 years old, my mother told me that while I was still in the womb, she spent six days in the hospital considering whether to have an abortion because doctors had told her there was a possibility that I would have the same problems Marcelo did. I understood at this time that this was one of the reasons why a demonic spirit found legality to attack me making me feel rejected, unloved and excluded on a deep subconscious level.

When I was six or seven years old, my father decided to leave home. For my mother, that was liberating. Until then, she hadn't truly lived. I believe that she felt bad about his departure, yet it also brought her relief. She was finally able to pursue her own dreams, which until then had seemed dead.

For me, my father leaving was heart-breaking because even with all the hurt, he was my father, and he was abandoning us. He was a hero to me. I loved it when he took me to barbecues, parties, and bars. It meant so much to me when he bought me a soft drink and a snack. After all, kids are innocent. I was so proud when my father's friends said I was like my father. Sometimes, I drank a little bit of beer with my father. All these experiences were openings in my soul for demons to enter.

From that point on, I began to have terrible manifestations during the night. Sometimes, I woke up hopeless, trembling like I was running away from something chasing me. I remember the images that I saw in the night: faces that came to my mind to scare me, someone running after me. I tried to escape, but I woke up, and the images continued because they were not simply a dream. I would run around the house, shouting and trembling. I climbed onto the furniture, sweating and shouting. I think that my mother – desperate and not knowing what to do – prayed for me.

After my father left us, we went to live in a small house that my uncle found for us. A cousin lived in the back, and he sometimes sexually abused me. This caused a lot of confusion in my mind. For a while, the evil spirit harassing me said I should be a woman. But I fought against that. The demonic spirits were pressing on me.

For part of the time when I was a child, I was raised by my paternal grandmother. Thia is because my mother had to take my brother

Marcelo to many places for treatment for his mental problems. It was a lot of work. Marcelo lived in a little room; he was practically imprisoned. My grandmother taught my older brother and me the Catholic traditions and doctrines. That's why I visited the Catholic church and attended mass at least once a month. There was within me a need to seek God. I remember that well!

As I grew up, all these experiences shaped my life. When I was a teenager, I started drinking alcohol. I struggled with many internal conflicts. I felt inferior and didn't think I could be someone worthwhile. I always felt insignificant. I believed that my destiny was to die very early. I thought my path was to drink, use drugs, and lead an immoral life. I decided to live in a completely worldly way. I tried smoking, but I didn't get the hang of it. I was best at drinking. I was very proud of how much alcohol I could drink, sometimes more than my older cousins. I didn't realize it at the time, but I wanted to be just like my father. The same spirit that dominated him was dominating me. Today, I have forgiven my father and pray that he will be converted to Jesus. I visit him every year at his house.

One day I was invited to participate in a youth meeting at the Methodist Church. After that, I began to attend worship there. It was at that church that I experienced Christ and was freed from the evil spirits. They left, and the chains were broken. But before that, I spent a year attending church.

One day during the time of the carnival festival, which is a folkloric and typical Brazilian festival that takes place every year in the month of February. Where it is also known as the festival of the flesh since these festivals involve a lot of drinking, drugs and promiscuity. I was walking home after a service with a brother from church. He walked far ahead of me. When I saw he wasn't returning, I went to the city center to go to a dance. While there, I drank more than most people. The security guards took me out twice because I was involved in disturbances. Back inside the club, the Lord spoke to me, saying, "Son, this is not your place. Leave." I heard God's voice and responded.

Things began to happen. My pastor helped me start to read the Bible. I received the baptism of the Holy Spirit. I realized that I received spiritual gifts, although I did not know what they were. Everything was changing in my life.

My experience with the Holy Spirit was tremendous. I was at a retreat called the Great Encounter, where there were people of all ages and from different churches. American missionaries were ministering at the meeting. I was staying at the university, happy to be with adults as I earnestly sought God. We were all praying together under some trees when a man I didn't know hugged me and started praying with me. At that moment, my legs went numb, and I fell to the ground. I was caught up in the Spirit and could see the glory of God. It was wonderful! When I opened my eyes, I had the distinct sense that the heavens were open in front of my eyes.

This experience changed the direction of my life. From that point on, I began to pray for others, and they, too, began to receive the same anointing. Today, I realized that the Lord was baptizing me, giving me the gifts of the Spirit, and calling me to ministry.

We left that retreat and visited other groups. We prayed for people, and they received the powerful presence of the Holy Spirit.

God was confirming my call to ministry. One day, a woman saw me playing the drums in worship and told me that I would be a pastor. I never imagined that! Another day, I was seated in front of the Methodist Church in Cambará, and I felt the desire to be a pastor. Much later, I was at college and pastoring my home church.

My first experience in casting out a demon happened in my first year studying theology at Londrina. I was at the church where I had worked as a missionary; a man came to pick up his niece and manifested a violent evil spirit. At that moment, I had to pray and expel it. Despite being in my first year of seminary, people already called me "Pastor," so I felt obligated to cast out the demon. I don't remember exactly what happened, but I knew that prayer in the name of Jesus had the power to overcome demonic spiritual authorities.

Another result of that incident was the impact it had on my older brother, Wellington, who had come to visit us to attend the Church service that I was serving. He was not yet converted to Jesus and was dominated by bad habits. He saw that demonic manifestation and it made a great impression on him. He was terrified. The Holy Spirit began working in his life, and he was converted to Christ. Today, he is a leader in the church.

That experience set me on the journey toward deliverance ministry. For three years, the Theology seminary classes.  I don't remember attending any classes on the subject, but God was preparing me. I felt the desire to be an instrument in the hands of the Lord, to do the work of the ministry, and to preach the gospel.

While I was in college, I never stopped working at the church and was always preaching and helping pastors. Early on Friday mornings, we would go to a hill to pray. We sought the fire of the Spirit and the vision of God so that the flame would never go out and God would guide us. A college friend of mine was involved in ministry, and I was amazed at how powerfully God used him. I wondered: Why did it not happen to me yet?

When I moved to become a pastor in the region of Paraná and Santa Catarina, Brazil, God started to work through me and still does so today. The Lord has given me tremendous experiences with people who need spiritual deliverance. In this journey, I have learned, through the Bible and spiritual experience, some simple and practical things. I want to share those with you now.

# Chapter 2

# Demons Know Who the Authority Is

*"What do you want with us, Son of God?" they shouted. "Have you come here to torture us before the appointed time?"*

*- Matthew 8:29*

The demons knew who they were in the presence of the Son of God. Ironically, the religious Jews did not recognize Jesus. On the contrary, when Jesus delivered a blind and speech-impaired man from the demons, He was accused by the Pharisees of casting out demons as the prince of demons *(Matthew 12:22-24).*

*James 2:19* says that even "demons believe and fear." In fact, they know more about spiritual authority than many Christians do. This is why many Christians and ministries are defeated; we cannot obey an authority we do not recognize. Demons know who the authority is. But they do not obey because they choose rebellion.

*Acts 19:13-15* are an example of spiritual authority in action. The sons of Sceva were traveling exorcists who tried to cast out demons one day by imitating what they saw Christians do: refer to Jesus. But the demons replied that they knew Jesus and they knew Paul, but they didn't know the sons of Sceva. That encounter didn't end well for Sceva's boys.

Many people have appointed themselves to ministries: "I am the deliverer." "I am an apostle," "I am a missionary." "I am a pastor," and so on. The truth is demons know who has delegated authority.

In *Acts 13*, the demons knew Jesus had the ultimate authority. And they knew that the Apostle Paul had delegated authority from Jesus Himself. In *Acts 9*, God gave Paul a ministry. Paul never considered designating himself as an apostle. On the contrary! He admitted that he persecuted the Church, but he stated that he was an apostle by the will of God.

In deliverance, it is crucial that we remain humble and never put ourselves in a position. Authority must be delegated by God and be confirmed by the church and the leadership God set up.

I have seen many come into the deliverance ministry because they like having to the attention. Sometimes, they believe themselves to be better than their pastor, better than their leader. That attitude causes division in many churches because the person begins to see some results in ministry and then falls to the temptation of vanity and rebellion. The demons that they were casting out turn around and capture them. The ministry is overshadowed by rebellion and division.

If God called and qualified you for a particular ministry, He Himself will confirm it. You don't need to force anything. Your opportunities will come as long as you place your future in the hands of the Lord. The scripture says that casting out demons will be a sign that will accompany all who believe *(Mark 16:7)*. In 1 Corinthians 12:9, there is talk of the *gifts* (plural) of healing because there are many types of diseases, and some people are used more often for the cure of particular diseases than others. I believe deliverance is a spiritual healing.

Often, the healing of lives tormented by demonic spirits will be given to those who have gifts of healing. In short, some will be called to exercise this ministry, but this does not mean that they are superior to those who have other gifts. Those who pray for deliverance need to be under authority. Moreover, no one who refuses to be under authority can continue in this ministry.

Anyone can see manifestations of demons. But deliverance can only be carried out by the one who truly has spiritual authority and discernment. In **Luke 8**, the demonic manifestations in the region of the Gerasenes were seen by all. Likewise, in **Matthew 17:15,** the demons caused the boy to fall into the fire and into the water.

We are not to pray to see demonic manifestations but to pray for deliverance. Even rebellious people may pray in the name of Jesus and see demons manifest themselves because of the power of Jesus' name. But the oppressed are not truly free. The person who is working in the ministry of deliverance needs to be released. Many people fear when they see a manifestation, and it can happen anywhere. But what God really wants is the complete deliverance of those who are enslaved by the enemy.

In the case of the sons of Sceva, demons manifested themselves, but the people were not delivered. The "deliverers" ended up being defeated by the demons. A lesson: rebellious people seeking to carry out deliverance ministry open themselves up to become the targets of demonic attack.

During one ministry time, I directed a woman to stop laying hands on others because I knew that she was unrepentant of her sinful lifestyle. But she ignored me and approached a young woman for whom I was praying at the time. I was indignant. How could she be so rebellious? The oppressed young woman seeking prayer was clearly bound by the power of darkness. As I prayed for her, the demonic spirit came out of her and entered the rebellious person who had been attempting to pray for her. I will never forget that extraordinary moment.

Another time, I was asked to pray for a woman in a nearby city who was imprisoned by evil spirits. She was staying as an invited guest at a pastor's house. The pastor was single and sick. When I arrived, I perceived that the people did not trust that pastor. The women of the church were taking his position of authority, treating him disrespectfully. These women could not cast out that demon. I ministered to everyone, telling them that they should honor the authority of the pastor. I asked the people and the pastor to authorize me to pray with the oppressed woman. The pastor prayed with me, and the devil was cast out in Jesus' name. Demons respect the church's designated authorities more than many Christians do.

Demons submit because they are forced to do so. Christians are to submit because they choose to do so out of love. This is clear in *James 4:7:* "So submit to God. Resist the devil, and he will flee from you." It is an unbreakable spiritual principle: I submit to God and to delegated authorities, and I can resist the devil. In the realm of darkness, the subject of authority is taken seriously. Demonic spirits only obey those who have authority. When accused of casting out demons by the spirit of Beelzebub (literally "Lord of the Flies" in Hebrew and the superior of demons), Jesus said, "If

Satan is divided against himself, how can his kingdom stand?" *(Luke 11:18).*

Notice that Jesus implies that the kingdom of darkness is organized. Evil spirits have limits in their work and cannot go beyond what they are authorized to do. They obey when a delegated authority gives a word of order.

Another experience that influenced me happened when I was invited to pray for a girl who was tormented by evil spirits. When I arrived at the house, three people were in the kitchen trying to hold her down. As soon as I stepped foot in the kitchen, she broke free, looked at me, and ran out into the street. I went after her. I followed from a distance and then gave a word of command from afar. She was thrown to the ground into a vacant lot. She remained on the ground, twisting like a snake. She gouged the ground with her hands. Family members then arrived to witness what was happening. I cast out the demons and right there in the street, everyone witnessed the glory of God. We returned to the house where there were many people. I asked if anyone wanted to accept Jesus. Everyone quickly raised their hands.

Demons must obey the authorities that the Lord delegates because they represent all that Jesus did on the cross. Those in authority represent and bear the marks of Jesus, and evil spirits must acknowledge them.

# Chapter 3

# Jesus Overcame and Makes Us Overcomers

When I began working with the ministry of deliverance, many people warned me that I would have to worry about retaliation and counterattacks from the devil. That put fear in my heart, and I became anxious. I wondered if I should continue working with this ministry and put my family at risk. One person told me that he heard a leader say that many of his church's members got sick after he started doing deliverance ministry.

I began to search the Word of God about this to understand that if Jesus delegated us to do the ministry, we don't need to be afraid of the counterattack. As I read the Word and prayed continually, I perceived that this fear was also Satan's strategy. He wanted to ignite fear in me so that I would stop ministering. As Christians, we face the tricks of Satan even when we do not work in deliverance.

**1 Peter 5:8** says, "Your adversary, the devil, prowls around like a roaring lion, seeking someone to devour."

Satan is going to fight against those who believe in Jesus. I understood that we could only be on one of two sides in this battle. We are either dominated by the devil, the empire of darkness, dead in our sins and trespasses, and under the feet of the devil to be trampled by him, or we are in the kingdom of God's beloved Son, redeemed from all sin, and washed with the blood of the Lamb, stepping on the devil's head.

In **Luke 10:19,** Jesus gives the disciples the authority to trample on snakes and scorpions and all the power of evil. We need to believe that the Lord has given us this authority.

We do not need to be afraid to do deliverance ministry because the same God who called us is the one who empowers us and gives us victory. Overcoming the enemy does not depend on what I am feeling at the time because what I feel does not change the reality that in Christ, I am more than an overcomer.

*Colossians 2:14-15* revealed to me that my life was hidden in Christ. We overcome the power of Satan because Christ defeated the principalities and powers on the cross. Christ exposed them to contempt and triumphed over them on Calvary's cross. Christ, like a Roman general, celebrated victory over the enemy, binding him and taking away all the weapons he had against us. If we are in Christ, the enemy has no weapons against us. He must fall and retreat because his most powerful weapon is accusation. But we are redeemed through Jesus' blood shed on the cross. The debt which was against us was removed and cancelled. When Satan looks at us, he sees the blood of Jesus and cannot touch nor destroy us. He cannot come against those who are covered by the blood.

*Revelation 12:10-11* says that Satan accuses believers day and night, but he was overcome because of the blood of the Lamb.

Christ's victory becomes our victory, and we need to believe in the power of what the Lord Jesus did on the cross. I learned that Christians need to be under this blood every day, obeying what the word says in *1 John 1:9,* "If we confess our sins, He is faithful and just to forgive us our sins and to cleanse us from all unrighteousness." For if we confess to God every day, humble ourselves and acknowledge our mistakes, we take possession of the victory Jesus won on the cross. Then, when Satan tries to accuse us, he will not have ground to stand on.

The problem is that many believers fail to confess their sins because they are not truly repentant. They are convinced that they have done nothing wrong. They are hard-hearted, unable to be honest with the Lord and fail to recognize their own mistakes. There is no conviction of sin in their hearts. They justify their sins. They say, "I was wrong because of my husband…" or "I did wrong because of my wife..." This is like Adam and Eve, who tried to hide from God and placed the blame on each other *(Gen. 3:12-13).*

Or some believers can think," I'm not so bad," and they try to make up for their sins by their own effort. But *Isaiah 64:6* says, "…our righteous acts are like filthy rags; we all shrivel up like a leaf, and like the wind, our sins sweep us away".

This deception leads to bondage for many. They are not reconciled with God; they hide, and they do not recognize their mistakes. They do not have a broken heart like the Apostle Paul did in

***Romans 7:24*** when he cried out, "Wretched man that I am! Who will deliver me from this body of death?" As a result, they do not find the victory. Paul expressed a few verses later in chapter 8:1, "There is therefore now no condemnation for those who are in Christ Jesus." This is the secret to victory: to be hidden in Christ and sensitive to the Holy Spirit, always with a repentant heart and open to the Lord's corrections. Then, we will be ready to trample snakes and scorpions.

# Chapter 4

# The Lord Gives Us Authority and Protection

In *Mark 16:17-18*, the Lord says, *"And these signs will accompany those who believe: In my name they will drive out demons; they will speak in new tongues; they will pick up snakes with their hands; and when they drink deadly poison, it will not hurt them at all; they will place their hands on sick people, and they will get well."*

If the Lord sent us to do the work, He would protect us. He is faithful and able to keep us safe. God will not allow the enemy to touch us or destroy us for working in deliverance.

I experienced this myself. I had the privilege of having a daughter with special needs. I say "privilege" because, through her, we have seen the greatness and sovereignty of God daily.

When I was carrying a heavy load of deliverance ministry in the church, my daughter was going through a terrible illness. She suffered from up to three violent epileptic seizures per day.

Once, while ministering to people at the altar, my daughter suffered a seizure in the church yard. When a child came running and said: "Pastor, María Fernando died." I was super scared, but it wasn't true. The boy didn't know that when she had a seizure, she would fall wherever she was. Some insinuated that this illness was because my ministry was bothering the devil. I was filled with fear until I took hold of the Word of God and conquered those fears.

The enemy always tries to keep us from putting our faith in the Word of God. He wants to confuse us and lead us away from a correct understanding of the divine teachings. Satan even tried this with Jesus. After Jesus spent 40 days in the wilderness, he quoted the scripture to try to tempt Jesus. But Jesus overcame that strategy by having confidence in the correct understanding of God's Word. The enemy attacks our minds so that we believe more in his power than in God's Word. When we entertain this thinking, we allow disbelief to enter our hearts.

So, when my daughter was having convulsions, I took hold of the victory of the Word and continued to minister even though my daughter was having convulsions. Doctors told us that she would never be able to stop taking the medicine and that she would always have seizures. We gave her medicine for two years, hoping that would make the seizures less severe. But as we took hold of God's promises, she never had a seizure again. She was cured. At one point, he was taking 13 medications a day.

Today, he does not take any medication and has never had seizures for the last 21 years. The enemy is always trying to prevent us from taking possession of what was already granted to us by the death of Christ on the cross. Try to sow doubts in God's promises. For example, in *Matthew 17:14-21*, the disciples tried and failed to cast out a demon. The demon-possessed child's father told Jesus about what was happening. Jesus clearly expected His disciples to be able to cast out this demon because He replied, "O faithless and perverse generation! How long shall I be with you? How long shall I bear with you?" Then Jesus cast out the demon. He later instructed His disciples, saying that this type of demon was cast out with fasting and prayer.

The Twelve did not yet know how to enjoy the glorious and powerful presence of the Master Jesus. This was out of disbelief.

Jesus was saying that the disciples needed to fast and pray, not to earn the right to receive authority. But because fasting and prayer increase intimacy with God, they will consequently bring an increase in faith, decreasing the unbelief that hinders our ability to manage complicated cases.

# Chapter 5

# Conquering Fear

One of the enemy's most powerful weapons is fear. Many believers are afraid of the devil; they don't even want to talk about deliverance.

I know what fear feels like. Once, a woman came up to me during Sunday School and told me that the evil spirit had told her that I was afraid of him. I later learned that the mother of this woman who approached me was a witch, so with this, she opened the doors for her daughter to be possessed by demons. I thought about her words all day. The Holy Spirit prompted me to read the scriptures, which reminded me that the only one who is omniscient, omnipresent, and omnipotent is the Lord God and no one else *(Psalm 91 and Psalm 139)*. I claimed the Word of the Lord, which says, *"There is no fear in love. But perfect love drives out fear because fear has to do with punishment. The one who fears is not made perfect in love (1 John 4:18).* I believed what the Holy Spirit was saying to me. Later that Sunday night, that woman came to the service, and during the prayer time, she came forward and stood in front of me.

When I started to pray for her, she immediately took off her jacket and fell to the ground. She was freed from that evil spirit that possessed her. Others later told me that before coming to our church, she had gone to a different one, and during that prayer time, she had taken off almost all her clothes at the altar, but she was not delivered. But thank God, on this day, she was delivered from the power of evil and the glory of the Lord was displayed.

We don't need to be afraid. We need to be alert, fear God, obey the Lord, trust His Word, seek sanctification, and praise and worship the Lord. And we do not need to be afraid to talk about the subject of demons or to order them to get out of our way. We don't need to surrender anything that is ours or let him steal anything from us. Jesus told us that *"the thief comes to kill, to steal, and to destroy" (John 10:10).* But Jesus came to give us life in abundance. We need to claim that life, believe in it, and pursue it wholeheartedly.

The Apostle Paul was clear about the spiritual battle we are engaged in. He says that we must put on all the armor of God *(Ephesians 6:10-17).* The armor incudes the shield of faith, the sword of the Spirit, the helmet of salvation, the breastplate of righteousness, the belt of truth, and the shoes of the gospel of peace. These are essential to defeating the enemy and overcoming the fear the devil wants to impose on us. The helmet protects the mind; the sword of the Word of God allows us to attack; the shield of faith protects us against the fiery darts of the evil one; the breastplate of righteousness guards the heart; the belt of truth frees us from the shame of lies; and the gospel of peace lets us walk without stumbling.

As we learn to put on this armor, we will no longer be dominated by fear because we are no longer guided by our soul or by our feelings but by the Spirit of God. God will lead us, and although we sometimes feel fear, we must place ourselves on the altar of God. He will be faithful to free us from all fear.

We cannot live by the feelings of the soul alone. Too many Christians are dominated by the soul -- or the flesh. They are dominated by their feelings. If their soul is sad, they doubt that Jesus is present with them. If they are joyful, they believe that Christ is with them. But the truth is Christ is always with us, whether we feel it or not. In *Matthew 28:20*, we read: *"And surely I am with you always, to the very end of the age."*

In fact, the conviction of Christ's presence is essential to overcome the temptations of the enemy. If we are confident, we can exercise authority. We do not allow the attacks of the enemy who tries to tell us that we are not important, that we are not special, or that we are losers.

If we are dominated by the soul, we are defeated. But by the Spirit of God, nothing can destroy us. Jesus was led and filled with the Spirit of God. When He began His ministry, He declared, *"The Spirit of the Lord is upon me" (Luke 4:18).* Jesus was led into the wilderness by the Spirit, and thanks to the Spirit's leading, He was able to overcome the enemy. Notice how the enemy attacked Him, wanting to influence His feelings. Satan starts by saying, *"If you are the Son of God..."*

Satan wants Jesus to doubt that He is truly loved or accepted by the Father. If Jesus had been influenced by the soul, He could have been open to doubt. He would have been resentful and deflated. But no! Jesus was convinced that God loved Him as a Son, for when Jesus was baptized the Spirit Himself had declared, *"You are my beloved son; in You I am well pleased." (Luke 3:21-22).*

We need to be led by the Spirit of God if we are to overcome the enemy. Many Christians today are just sentimental. If they are pleased with a church, they stay. If not, they don't stay. They do not ask: What is the will of the Spirit? They are looking for places and people that feed their ego or raise their self-esteem. But the Lord's goal is not to raise our self-esteem; He wants us to learn to deny ourselves.

At the end of His earthly ministry, Jesus had an even fiercer battle than the one in the wilderness. It happened in the Garden of Gethsemane when he asked the Father to take away the cup that represented the crucifixion. Jesus' soul was in anguish. He suffered to obey and subdue His flesh (Luke 22:39-46). No human being would go to the cross smiling with joy, knowing his hands would be nailed to wood and a crown of thorns would be placed on his head or that he would be humiliated, stepped on, and punished for his transgressions. But Jesus was facing that, and He was under so much stress that He sweat blood. Jesus' soul was suffering, yet He battled against the feelings of his soul and flesh to defeat the enemy. Satan, like Christians dominated by the feelings of the soul. Led by their feelings, they are easy prey-- easily tempted, deluded, deceived, and trampled.

In the end, the enemy has no weapons. He tries to convince us to give him the weapons to use against us by appealing to our flesh. When we crucify our flesh with Christ, we can walk in the Spirit and never satisfy the pleasures of the flesh *(Galatians 5:16)*. Victory comes from the cross and from dying to self.

Some want a ministry of deliverance as a way of promoting themselves. I have been approached by people who have asked me how to get into the ministry of deliverance. Our motivation cannot be to see supernatural manifestations to feel powerful. We need to love people and want to deliver them. We are not to desire a ministry of deliverance but rather to help people out of darkness. It is a tragedy when people who received the gift of healing do not allow God to heal their own fleshly nature.

When that happens, there is division, power struggles, and confusion and the glory of God is not revealed. True liberation will not happen only through liberating prayer but when there is discipleship, which will allow the person to know the truth. They need to see the deliverance minister as an example to follow. They need a disciple who not only prays to liberate but also lives a liberating life.

# Chapter 6
## Discipleship & Deliverance

*I pray that out of his glorious riches he may strengthen you with power through his Spirit in your inner being, so that Christ may dwell in your hearts through faith. And I pray that you, being rooted and established in love.*

*- Ephesians 3:16-17*

It has been my practice to challenge people who are in bondage to seek deliverance. We seek the Lord and pray for these people to become free from the chains of darkness. But after we pray for deliverance, we continue to assist people. They may have many things to renounce, confess, and repair. The person, or their parents, may have given the devil the right to interfere with their life. These need to be identified and placed on the altar of the Lord. If that is not done, the demons can manifest themselves during worship or even leave but then return because there are still open doors into the person's life.

On one occasion, I went to pray for a woman who had a physical manifestation of a demon. I asked the demon where he was getting access to her life. He answered, "Through the door."

Demons enter through open spiritual doors. We need to help the person identify the doorway demons are using to enter. Then, we urge the person to confess and renounce those open doors. We encourage them to claim the blood of Jesus and be purified of all sins so the curse is broken. From that point, we start to disciple the person. We teach the Word of God to destroy what is false and to build what is true. This cleanses the spirit and allows them to be filled with the knowledge of God's Word. Knowing the truth brings complete deliverance. Prayer, casting out the devil, renunciation, and confession of sins are part of deliverance.

*"And ye shall know the truth, and the truth shall make you free" (John 8:32).*

The second most important step is the opening for the Word of God to dwell in the heart, producing a genuinely healthy and fruitful Christian.

In *Matthew 12:43-45*, Jesus told us that if the demonic spirit that was expelled returns and sees that the house (person's spirit) is empty, it returns and brings seven worse spirits with it. The "house" – that is, a person's spirit – needs to be filled with the Word of God and the presence of the Holy Spirit. That happens through discipleship. That is why all deliverance work needs to be followed up with discipleship. People need to be in a class, Bible school, or small group and be accompanied by and accountable to someone with more experience.

Perhaps they could be discipled directly by a pastor or lay leader. Whatever approach we take, we must ensure that the person is accompanied by someone who can assist in their release. We cannot think that it is enough to expel the demon from the person during the time of prayer. In fact, this moment is where this person's liberation process begins. It is vital for that person to have significant support so that he can become completely freed and work fruitfully for the Lord.

# Chapter 7

# Deliverance Ministry Is Not Optional

*The Spirit of the Lord is on me because he has anointed me to proclaim good news to the poor. He has sent me to proclaim freedom for the prisoner and recovery of sight for the blind, to set the oppressed free.*

*-Luke 4:18*

I cannot afford to say that deliverance ministry is not for me. I've heard Christians say that casting out demons is not "their thing." Yes, there are people with the gift of healing who exercise that ministry more effectively than others do. But every Christian should be prepared to perform the ministry of deliverance, for when Jesus began His ministry, He declared that He came to set captives free *(Luke 4:18)*.

In *Mark 16:17, And these signs will accompany those who believe: In my name they will drive out demons; they will speak in new tongues; ... "* Jesus passed this ministry on to his disciples and to the Church. He did not say that in the future this work will no longer be needed.

Sometimes, a leader will specialize in deliverance ministry. He will need to pray for the Lord to raise up someone in his church with the needed spiritual gift because countless people who are dominated by demons go to church. Too often, they leave as they enter because there is no one doing the work of deliverance.

As I said earlier, it is not enough to cast out the demon and then leave the person to manage by themselves. It is not enough to stay connected to the person without driving out the demon that oppresses them. Many are tired and overloaded in ministry because they are trying to convince people to be open to change. What they don't know is that they are trying to convince and internally heal people who are full of demons. In this way, they cannot be effective in their work. This generates a lot of fatigue. It is necessary to expel the demon first and cleanse the spirit of the person with prayer and lead him or her to renounce and confess any sins. At this point begins the discipleship work that leads to inner healing.

The devil does what he can to prevent a person from paying attention to the Word of God. The enemy is tying people to the church pew, imprisoning them in a spirit of religiosity. This means that they may be very active in the work of the church, but they are not spiritually free. As a result, they obstructed the church's mission because they were not completely free from the chains that held them when they arrived. They may have believed that by attending church, everything would be resolved. But it is not so.

It is necessary to focus and invest in the oppressed person and to let that be known. This requires spiritual discernment. Those in the ministry of intercession and those in the ministry of deliverance are vital to the church because the devil stays hidden even as he follows people wherever they go.

We must be careful when people who are still in spiritual bondage get baptized and assume leadership positions in the church. I remember the case of a woman who was a leader of intercession. During a meeting, she manifested a demon, and everyone was amazed. Later, her pastor told me that she was one of the biggest gossipers in the church. I discerned that this woman was in spiritual chains and was involved in witchcraft. No one was delivered through her. She caused many problems in the mission of the church.

A spiritually delivered Christian is one who bears fruit, who is involved in the work of the gospel, and who is producing for God. There are many churches that cannot advance their missionary work because Satan's chains are binding the people and even the leadership. The Bible tells us that Jesus called Judas a devil *(John 6:70),* and Judas was one of The Twelve! Judas was negatively influencing the ministry. We see this when Mary anointed Jesus' feet with an expensive perfume called nard *(John 12:3).*

Judas criticized that gesture of love and self-denial. He displayed a false concern for the poor. The truth is, he was motivated by the father of lies. He was dominated by darkness. It is possible that people who are in the leadership of the church can act like Judas and hinder the mission. They block missionary investments or projects because Satan is preventing their growth. It is essential to work with those people and bring them deliverance from the chains of darkness.

The church needs to think about deliverance and work with the people. In some churches, we hear a lot of psychology and theory, but there is little of the power of God to deliver. The power of God is essential for the kingdom of God to be manifested. When Jesus was questioned about his liberating people, He said that demons were being cast out because the kingdom of God was manifesting. *"But if I cast out demons by the Spirit of God, surely the Kingdom of God has come upon you" (Matthew 12:28).*

People do not need theories; they need the power of God. And that is displayed in the gospel (Romans 1:16). When people encounter God through the power of the gospel, they find everything they need. The truth is we need to love God and have an encounter with Him. Nothing can substitute for the powerful presence of the Holy Spirit.

The gospel is enough to heal, liberate and restore human beings completely. However, there is a spiritual battle. Many people with paranormal visions transform liberation into something very complicated. However, the release is very simple! It is the Lord transferring us from the empire of darkness and into the kingdom of the Son who He loves. People are saved when they recognize their fallen nature and accept Jesus Christ as their only and sufficient Lord.

Breaking curses is nothing more than the result of confessing and repenting from dead works. We become free when we decide to abandon our old life and misconceptions, which were dominated by Adamic nature. Adamic nature naturally attracts demons. For example, when we find an animal on the road that has been dead for several days, we see the carnage and decomposition and several vultures are attracted by the bad smell. What is repulsive for us is delicious food to them.

In the same way, demons are attracted by the carnage of human sin. They are attracted to rebellion, lies, and prostitution. In fact, they are the ones that tempt human beings to fall, promising us our favorite food. We overcome the enemy when we decide to cleanse our spirits by the blood of Jesus *(1 John 1:9).* A repentant Christian is a victor, for the enemy can no longer oppose him. Finally, the deliverance of people dominated by spirits is an integral part of the church's mission to save the world.

# Chapter 8

## Deliverance and the Mission of God

*"For this purpose, the Son of God was manifested, that He might destroy the works of the devil."*

*-1 John 3:8b*

I am passionate about church planting, and I have seen how important deliverance ministry is to start a new church. I have had the opportunity to preach in a variety of places, and I see that people are exactly as they were in Jesus' time: sheep without a shepherd, in need of the healing of deliverance and love. Deliverance ministry is God's way of gathering people. We invite people to be delivered, and churches are planted from there.

At the beginning of His ministry, Jesus quoted the prophet Isaiah: *"The Spirit of the Lord is upon me because He has anointed Me to preach the gospel to the poor; He has sent Me to heal the brokenhearted, to proclaim liberty to the captives and recovery of sight to the blind, to set at liberty those who are oppressed" (Luke 4:18).* In our ministry, we serve as ambassadors of God, proclaiming Jesus' message, communicating God's message to the world.

In the church of Laranjeiras, Brazil, in 2003, we began a growth project. For this, we moved to a new and spacious place. At that time the Lord spoke to me that we were planting a new church. This has been very true because the old Methodist Church there was more than 60 years old and in a very small temple. And God fulfilled His word, and today, this church has become another big denomination, and the traditional Methodist church returned with some of its members to the premises of the old temple. God began to act, and the ministry prospered. Later, we opened two new missions in the surrounding cities.

I have seen churches that value deliverance ministry grows and reach lost people. Sometimes, the mistake of many is to want to give doctrine and solid spiritual food to people who are dominated by evil spirits. This doesn't work; first, it is necessary to free the people.

Many people do not remain in the church because a deep work of deliverance from spirits was not done with them. This allows the enemy to influence them away from the path of Jesus. We need to attack the enemy with the Word and with prayer. *"The god of this age has blinded the minds of unbelievers so that they cannot see the light of the gospel that displays the glory of Christ, who is the image of God (2 Corinthians 4:4).*

People are often blinded in their minds and prevented from seeing the light of the gospel. We need to perform a shock treatment. It is necessary to invade the gates of hell and rescue the captives.

Deliverance ministers are the kingdom's special forces. They use weapons that are not physical but powerful in God.

We can plant a church anywhere through deliverance ministry. We challenge people to come to be healed and delivered. Afterward, they can grow through spiritual nourishment and the doctrine of God's Word. We must not offer standards and doctrines to people new to the church. We need to offer them bread and water. What moves me to do this ministry is to see how much we can help people and how many souls we can win through it. If we think biblically, all the people who are in the world are dead in their sins. Thus, all are in some way living in the dominion of darkness *(Ephesians 2:1-2).*

In this way, everyone needs deliverance to some degree. I say this because many Christians think that only people involved with black magic and sorcery need deliverance. That is not so. Everyone in the world needs spiritual liberation, for they are imprisoned by chains. For those who have been more deeply involved with Satanic activity, the manifestations will be more evident, and they will require a different type of ministry.

People with demonic spirits will display a variety of manifestations. Some who are held captive have no apparent manifestations at all. Those who have been involved with witchcraft may display visible or bizarre manifestations, depending on the type of demon that is binding them.

In the Bible, we see demons manifest in diverse ways. For example, Jesus expelled a demon from a woman who had been hunched over for many years *(Luke 13:10-17).* That demon was binding her to an illness. Of course, not every illness is caused by a demon. Many are purely physical and can be treated by physicians. God uses medicine to heal. At the same time, some illnesses cannot be diagnosed or cured medically.

So, there are some illnesses that are caused directly by the influence of demons, which are "spirits of illness" which can only be cured by prayer for deliverance. In Luke 13, Jesus gave a word of deliverance to the woman who was bent over for 18 years. He laid his hands on her and declared her free. Sometimes, the manifestation of the devil is violent.

In *Mark 5,* Jesus cast out a legion of demons from the Gerasene's man. These demons led him to wound himself and to walk among the tombs. There are demons that lead a person to self-harm or to self-destruction. These lead a person to vices, to prostitution, to anything that leads a person not to value their life, even to the point of suicide.

In *Mark 9:14-23*, a demon caused a boy to be mute. *(See also Luke 11:14.)* Though demons act in a variety of ways, their aim is to kill, steal, and destroy *(John 10:10).*

I have had the experience of praying for people who had spirits physically affecting them with various illnesses. Many of these cases started as a curse uttered by a foolish parent. We need to know this background when we minister deliverance. It is clear in the Bible that parents have authority over their children. Parents can bless or curse their children.

In this way, when the father curses, he opens the door to demonic spirits to act in the lives of his children, allowing them to be bound by spiritual chains. When the children grow up, those chains need to be dealt with so they can be set free. When those grown children meet Jesus, those open doors need to be renounced and shut. Today, many adults are tormented by spirits that are entered through resentment of their parents or through their reaction to painful events.

The manifestation that made the biggest impression on me happened at a youth encounter retreat in Siqueira Campos. I believe that at least 50 people had demonic manifestations during a time of prayer. It was very sad to see so many young people who had given demonic spirits permission to possess them, yet at the same time; it was wonderful to see the power of God reveal those demons.

During the prayer time, all intercessors were praying for people, each one in their own way. Then, I guided them to give a single word of command so that the demons would come out. We prayed in unison, and the Lord was glorified. In one way or another, all those young people had given an opening to the enemy through sin, past resentments, or some other means. Demons do not enter without permission. One pastor questioned whether those young people were from the church. I told him that they were, but what happened was that these young people were just living a religion. That is, they were in the church, but they were not really converted to the Lord because they are dominated by sin.

In the next chapter, we will look at the issue of unforgiveness, which is a common way people who claim to follow Jesus open themselves to demonic oppression and possession. They say, "I was born again. I am of God. The old things have already passed." But they have many things that did not pass away that torment and dominate them. We must seek to eliminate all spiritual opening to the demonic and say like Jesus: *"…for the prince of this world is coming. He has no hold over me…" (John 14:30).*

# Chapter 9
# Lack of Forgiveness

*Be kind and compassionate to one another, forgiving each other, just as in Christ God forgave you.*

*Ephesians 4:32*

Unforgiveness is one of the most common ways people open themselves up to evil spirits. I have seen people hold on to the roots of bitterness for years. **Hebrews 12:15** says that the root of bitterness creates problems both for the bitter person and for those around them. Many church people are spiritually chained because they have not been able to forgive those who hurt them. Past wounds have generated resentment that took root in their hearts. These roots create a barrier in their minds and hearts, which keeps them from enjoying the abundant life that the Lord Jesus has for them. Their communion with the Lord is disrupted, and that opens them up to the activity of evil spirits.

I once ministered to a lady who had been abandoned by her husband. She said she did not have any hard feelings, but it was clearly visible that she did. While praying, I had a vision that she was walking hunched over. The Lord was using an image of her physical appearance to reveal her spiritual condition: she was dominated by a demonic spirit that burdened her with a heavy yoke. When we prayed, she began to spit, which indicated the activity of demonic spirits in her.

It is usually very difficult for people to realize and admit that they harbor hatred, bitterness, and a desire for vengeance. Often, they deny it at first. But when they recognize and reject the bitterness, they can forgive and become open to the process of deliverance.

Once, I went to visit a gentleman who had cancer. He was a landowner and a farmer. Even though he was not a Christian, I was invited to visit him and pray for his healing. As I was talking with him, God showed me that he held a deep and powerful resentment toward someone. When I asked him about it, his face changed; his eyes blazed with hatred. I believe this reaction revealed the cause of his cancer. He hated an employee who had abused his granddaughter. We prayed for him, but he didn't want to forgive. This impeded his healing and deliverance process.

Another misconception about forgiveness that we need to combat is time. Many assume that time helps the process of forgiveness. However, the reality is that waiting only delays healing and deliverance. That is why the Apostle Paul teaches that we should not let the sun set on anger. Instead, when we get angry, we are to quickly forgive *(Ephesians 4:26).*

Waiting does not help. In fact, it hurts. Unforgiveness gives Satan the opportunity to act. In 2 Corinthians 2:10-11, the Apostle Paul urges the church to forgive a brother who had sinned against the community of believers so that Satan would not gain an advantage over them. What would result from this advantage? If the people did not forgive and continued to cultivate resentment, it would divide the church and cause dissension.

A story about cultivated hatred that caught my attention is found in Genesis 34. Jacob's daughter, Dinah, was visiting some of the women of the area when a man named Shechem attacked and humiliated her. When her brothers became aware of this, they were outraged. Shechem and his father proposed that Shechem marry Dinah and unite their families. Dinah's brothers pretended to accept the arrangement, but they were not being truthful. They said that they would only agree to the marriage if all the men of Shechem's town were circumcised. Shechem and his father accepted these terms. But three days later, when all the men of the town were in pain from circumcision, Dinah's brothers attacked and killed them all. This massacre and destruction all stemmed from the brothers' hatred and resentment. Unforgiveness generates a desire for revenge, destruction, and even death. That curses a home, family, and church.

Another gateway for demons to enter lives is guilt. How many people have not yet managed to feel forgiven by God? They carry the weight of their sin and are prisoners of the accuser, who accuses them day and night. They have not yet managed to appropriate the blood shed by Christ and the forgiveness granted by him. They live as prisoners of their past actions.

I remember a woman who hurt a couple a lot. When she was younger, the woman used witchcraft to make that couple miserable. It turns out that the couple has been tormented by an illness where their bodies were consumed, and they died. This had happened 30 years before the time she told me, and she had been part of a church for at least 20 of those years without finding peace. She served on the church's intercession team, praying and laying hands on many people, but she herself was always sick.

The day I prayed with her, she told me that she had never told that story to anyone and that she felt a lot of guilt about what had happened. She regularly heard a voice at night telling her that she was a murderer. When I started to pray with her, I did not lay hands on her, yet she was thrown more than five feet from a sofa into my office. She fell on the floor with her hands drawn back; her eyes were rolled back in her head. She was manifesting an evil spirit. I was able to minister the forgiveness of God to her and lead her to take hold of the forgiveness that is in Jesus, whose blood was shed on the cross for us all.

I want to emphasize the importance of the blood of Jesus. It purifies us from all sin as we confess and repent *(1 John 1:9).* If we hide from the truth and do not admit the wrong things we have done, we will feel guilt, pain, and heaviness. And we are open ourselves to the attack of the enemy. We need to appropriate the blood of Jesus that was shed for our freedom.

***Revelation 12:11*** says it is through the blood of Jesus that we have victory against the accuser. The blood of Jesus justifies us before God. The blood purifies us; that is, the stain of sin is extinguished, and God rejoices. The blood of Jesus protects us from the attacks of the enemy, for when the destroyer sees the blood, he cannot hurt us. In the book of Exodus, the tenth plague upon the Egyptians was for the firstborn to die. Yet the destroyer could not enter the Israelites' houses if the blood was sprinkled on the thresholds of the doors *(Exodus 11:1-10).* You and I must appropriate the blood of Jesus through confession. That will set us free from all guilt, and we will be freed from all the burdens imposed by the enemy. *"There is therefore now no condemnation to those who are in Christ Jesus..." (Romans 8:1)*. This is our faith. We need to cultivate this trust.

# Chapter 10
# The Fire of God

Throughout the Bible, one of the ways God chooses to manifest Himself is through fire. In Genesis, when the Lord made a covenant with Abraham, He manifested Himself in a "smoking firepot with a blazing torch." Our God is indeed a God of fire. In the destruction of Sodom and Gomorrah, God manifested Himself with the fire of judgment because of the cities' wickedness *(Genesis 15:17; Genesis 19:24)*.

Also, in Exodus, when God calls Moses to deliver the people from the slavery of Egypt, he manifests Himself as fire that burned a bush, but it did not burn down *(Exodus 3:2)*. When Solomon consecrated the newly built temple, "fire came down from heaven and consumed the burnt offering and sacrifices, and the glory of the Lord filled the temple" *(2 Chronicles 7:1)*.

When Elijah confronted the prophets of Baal on Mount Carmel, God's presence and power were displayed when fire consumed the offerings and the pagan priests *(1 Kings 18:38)*.

Some of the other manifestations of God's fire in the Old Testament include the fire that consumes the sacrifice on the altar which the priests should not let go out *(Leviticus 6:8-13)*. It is the fire of the glory of the Lord that reveals the power of a God who does not lie.

*Deuteronomy 4:24* says, *"For the Lord, your God is a consuming fire, a jealous God."* Sometimes, the manifestations of God's fire in the Old Testament brought blessings. At other times, it brought judgment. The truth is the fire of God does not change; what changes is where He manifests Himself and upon whom He manifests Himself. For example, for Elijah, the fire was a manifestation of blessing and victory; for the prophets of Baal, it was destruction and judgment. In the same way as Sodom and Gomorrah, for the family of Lot, it was freedom; for the sinful cities and their inhabitants, it was total destruction. The fire of God means blessing, life, and peace for those who obey the Lord, while it brings judgment for those who rebel.

God manifested Himself as fire in the New Testament as well. On the day of Pentecost, the Holy Spirit descended upon the believers in the form of tongues of fire *(Acts 2:1-3).* John the Baptist announced that he would baptize with water, but someone more powerful than himself would come who would baptize with the Holy Spirit and fire *(Luke 3:16).* Fire is one of the most wonderful ways God manifests his presence because fire:

- Illuminates: it leads us on the right path; it does not allow us to stumble.

- Warm: it does not allow insensitivity or indifference.

- Burns: consumes, purifies, and destroys.

These traits of fire reveal why God chooses to manifest Himself this way. Like fire, the Heavenly Father lights our path, warms our hearts, and burns away all impurity. And His presence leaps from person to person (which we call discipleship.)

In my journey in the ministry of deliverance, I have understood and learned to use the power of God's fire. The fire of God brings blessings to His children but judgment to demons. I discovered that when I cry out for God's fire in moments of deliverance, I sense a prophetic anticipation of the fate of Satan and his demons, as described in

*"The devil, who deceived them, was cast into the lake of fire and brimstone where the beast and the false prophet are. And they will be tormented day and night forever and ever."*

*Revelation 20:10:*

Demons will be destroyed by the power of God's fire, which is nothing more than the manifestation of His presence. They are unclean, so they cannot bear the presence of the glory of the Lord. He is perfectly holy, and they are utterly impure, so it is impossible for them to have a relationship with God. So, when we cry out for fire, they are burned by the power of God, and they must leave the people they are oppressing.

When I cry out for fire, the demons manifest and must come out. Sometimes, we start to pray, and nothing happens. But we need to persevere in prayer and cry out for the fire of God. One time, I was praying for a woman who manifested many demons. They caused her to hit my arm. As soon as she did that, she began jumping and shouting, "It's burning, it's burning!" Demons cannot touch us without burning because we are revested with the fire of the Holy Spirit.

We need to learn this lesson: we do not need to touch to expel demons. We are not to use human force because if we do, we will lose. But if we operate in the power of the fire of God, the demons are defeated.

If a demon manifests aggressively, we need to give a command in the power of Jesus' name. Then, the demon will have to surrender. I have often witnessed demons wanting to talk or fight. But when I give the order, they are bound, blocked by the power of God's fire.

In one case, a girl responded to the call to prayer during the time of worship. There were many people at the altar alongside her. I began to pray for her, and demons manifested themselves. I thought: "All those people are here to receive the prayer, and if I go toward her now, I'm going to use up all my time, and the others will be left waiting." The Holy Spirit directed me: "Pray and give a command in the power of the Holy Spirit that the demon remains bound." When I gave the order, the girl stood paralyzed in a unique position for around 15 minutes until we prayed for everyone.

Then, I was able to go to her and dedicate more time to her deliverance. The enemy wanted to hinder worship and prayer for the sick, the new converts, and others. It is necessary to have wisdom so that we can act appropriately. The fire of God enlightens us, directing us to do the right things at the right time.

I was preaching in a church, and a girl began praying in strange tongues, as if she were a gift from God. In the same instant, the Holy Spirit told me, "Go to her and rebuke her." I left the altar and approached to place my hands on his head. It was a demon that was manifesting at the time, to prevent people from hearing the word of God. So, the Holy Spirit gave me the discernment to pray and rebuke. God's illuminating fire gives clarity like the gift of discernment of spirits does. Yet, the power of God's fire not only gives us discernment of spirits, but it also gives discernment in all areas of life *(1 Corinthians 12:10).* This gift is necessary because sometimes we minister to people who are simulating manifestations of demons.

Some time ago, I ministered to a woman who was screaming, "I'm not going out, I'm not going out." Some brothers had been praying for her for quite some time and were already tired. When I arrived and saw that situation, the Holy Spirit enlightened me and showed me that it was not a demon. I approached the woman and said in her ear, "You are going to stop screaming now and come back to hear the Word of God, and you are going to stop putting on a show here." She stopped screaming and returned to hear the Word of God. It was just a fleshly imitation of a manifestation of demons. The truth is demons must obey when we pray in the name of Jesus and in the power of the Holy Spirit's fire. They cannot say, "I will not go out," any more than it is possible for light to mix with darkness.

Demonic spirits bind people in specific areas. Some people are imprisoned in sexuality. They may have led a life of prostitution, adultery, or homosexuality. When praying for one young man, the Holy Spirit showed me that he was bound by demonic spirits, which led to a promiscuous life. I began to cry out for the fire of

God. Confronted with God's presence, the demon manifested by causing the young man to urinate himself as he fell to the floor. And the spirit was commanding his sexual organs because of the wicked relationships he was in. Satan bound him in chains, but when I cried out, the fire of God came with power and glory. Afterward, I asked everyone to leave the room. The pastors and I stayed there with him to embrace him and not allow him to be too ashamed.

Demons, no matter how hidden they may be, cannot resist the power of the Holy Spirit's fire. That is why we need to cry out for fire. I have been the butt of jokes because when I pray for deliverance, I begin to cry out: "Fire, fire, fire, fire!" However, I ignore that mocking. But I want to clarify that this type of prayer is not a new method. It is not a magic formula. It is a revelation from God in the Word about the power of the Holy Spirit's fire. It is of no use for someone who has not been filled with the Holy Spirit and His fire to pray for fire. First, we must be aflame with the fire. We cannot have the fire; the fire must have us.

Let me mention the ministry of angels in deliverance. "He makes his angels spirits, and His ministers a flame of fire" *(Hebrews 1:7)*. The text is referring to angels as servants of God.

The seraphim appear in the vision of the throne of Isaiah 6. According to the commentary in the Plenitude Bible study, seraphim in the plural are those who burn or barely burn; they can also be called agents that God uses for purification. When we cry out for the presence of God's fire, we recognize it has come by its purifying and cleansing away of all the filth that the presence of evil brings upon people. When angels are present, it is the presence of God that is doing the work. There are a lot of superstitions surrounding the subject of angels. We cannot directly ask angels to come, for the Bible teaches that they are ministers of God in the service to those who have inherited eternal life *(Hebrews 1:14).*

It is God who has power over them. It is God who determines where they will go and what they will do. In Psalms 91:11, we read: *"For He will command His angels concerning you to guard you in all your ways."* We cannot summon angels or give them orders. We need to ask God in Jesus' name to command His angels. In difficult deliverance cases, I have cried out to God to send specific angels to help, and He has sent angels, and the demons have submitted.

Yet, it is God who decides whether to command angels, not us. We can only appropriate the Bible's promise that He will ordain His angels for our service. Daniel 10 recounts a spiritual battle. From the day Daniel began to seek God, the angel was commanded to bring him the answer. But an opposing spirit prevented the answer from reaching Daniel. The text says that the angel Michael battled and prevailed over the spirit so that the answer could come. That is a vivid picture of the battle that takes place in the spiritual world. We need to learn to trust that God will give orders to His angels at the right time. Our role is to keep this promise and enjoy that blessing.

# Chapter 11
# The Missionary Vision

**"Ask me, and I will make the nations your inheritance, the ends of the earth your possession."**

*-- Psalms 2:8*

I have seen the glory of the Lord manifest, and I have learned, through obedience, to experience the miracles of the Lord. When I came to pastor the Methodist Church of Laranjeiras do Sul, Brazil, I was very sad because I was involved in a growth project in another church. We had just built a new worship facility, and I had many dreams for that place. But unfortunately, I could not stay for various reasons.

At times, I thought I had not been called to the ministry. At other times, I knew God had called me, but I thought about giving it up. As we were moving to that church, my beloved wife, Shirley, had just given birth to our son, Israel Rafá. But he couldn't go home; he was hospitalized in the neonatal ICU of the Evangelical Hospital of Londrina. We visited him weekly and had hopes of seeing him cured. We wanted to take him to the room that we had prepared for him. We lived 160 kilometers from Londrina. We could get there at any time. When we were appointed to Laranjeiras do Sul, we would be about 400 kilometers away. I would not get to visit him weekly.

As we were leaving Londrina, the Lord put a message into my heart and in Shirley's. We are offering Israel, just as Abraham offered Isaac. The only time we returned to Londrina was to do Israel's wake.

Through this situation, I learned that the Lord is sovereign and that He healed Israel by taking him away. Many times, I preached in Laranjeiras while thinking of Israel there in Londrina. I believe that the Lord always has the best for us, and all that sadness was transformed into a blessing as the church there welcomed me with much love and helped to confirm my ministry.

After I arrived at Laranjeiras, we welcomed brothers who came from Canada to do missionary work in the church and in the city. They came through Brother Charles – a Canadian native of Ivory Coast who came to play soccer in Cambará, Brazil. Charles began to attend our church. We became friends, and the dream of learning about Canada and preaching there was born.

In 2004, I had the opportunity to visit Canada and get to know a little about that country and to preach in some churches. I remember Pastor Israel's church in Montreal, where there were many manifestations of people who were tormented by spirits.

At the end of the meeting, a young man came to meet me and told me that they needed that ministry. I saw people who were considering suicide, screaming, crying, in anguish, and experiencing a lot of demonic oppression in their lives. Through the power of the Spirit, we were able to minister deliverance. The Lord did great things in that place.

Two years later, I had the opportunity to return to Canada to study French for a month and to preach. I did not master the language and placed myself in the hands of the Lord. I met a brother from Rio de Janeiro who had been living with a family in Montreal for three months, attending that church. The pastor challenged him to be a French translator. He accepted, so I was able to preach in two churches with an interpreter. Again, the Lord opened doors so that I could be used in that place. What I learned from that is when the Lord wants to use us, there are no barriers.

We did not intend to pray and wait for the Lord to open the doors for the mission in Canada. But I believe those visits and ministries were planned and directed by God. And as I write, I am on a quest to discover God's purpose for my ministry. I am certain that the Lord awakened an intense desire in my heart to do cross-cultural missions, to be able to meet and preach in many places in Brazil and in other nations, bringing the message of deliverance.

You are also part of this project of God. Be an intercessor and cooperator in God's mission to save the world.

We are living in the last days, so we need to rise as "a worker who does not need to be ashamed" who will preach the Word in season or out of season.

Brazil is a source of missionaries for the world. It is time for us to go to the countries where the Lord has opened the doors for missions. God will certainly give us victory in that project, for He promised that the gates of hell will not prevail against the church.

The mission needs to happen through us. We cannot be afraid of spiritual battles. We must enlist for this great ministry. If you have been called to the ministry of deliverance, do not be afraid. Look for God in your heart. Be willing to seek help from people who have more experience in this area, especially those who have been working in it for a long time. Begin to read God's Word, searching for guidance and understanding of deliverance. You will discover incredible revelations from the Lord on the subject. Do not think that because you are working in this ministry, you are better than your pastor or your leader. Submit humbly. Do not desire that things happen your way; let the Holy Spirit guide your steps.

Many have already asked me, "Did you ask to have gifts?" The truth is, I never asked for them, despite feeling the desire to have them for a long time. I simply submitted to the Lordship of Christ and His sovereign will, and He acted in me and through me. If the Lord wills, He Himself will guide you to the ministry of deliverance.

I remember once, I went to minister deliverance in a church for four days and nothing happened: no manifestation, no prayer for deliverance. Everything was quiet. Then on the last day, as I was leaving, I grabbed my Bible as I was walking out the door of the church, and a woman approached and said: "Pastor, can you pray with me? I was too embarrassed to go to the altar during the time of worship." I said, "Okay, if I can." As I began to pray with her, seven demons manifested. God is in control! He knows what He is doing! But when God wants to use your life, you do not need to force anything; things happen spontaneously.

I once went to a meeting to preach. I was not leading; I had just been invited to preach. At a certain point in the meeting, another colleague was ministering during the time of prayer when a demon manifested in a person. But I did not go beyond offering to cast out the demon. I really wanted to do it because I perceived that people were having difficulty working with that case. But I restrained my anxiety and my desire. I began to pray that God would use those who were praying and that if he wanted me to help, the leaders would call.

A few minutes passed, and someone came to call me. I went there, and we cast out that demon. She was a woman who had been raped by her father as a child. She was really dominated by demons for many years, and in that moment, the Lord delivered her from those spirits. Glory to God!

The true God is the one who supports with signs and wonders. The signs will be so clear that you do not need to force anything.

I once went to a house to pray for a man dominated by evil spirits. His wife said that when the devil manifested, she placed water in a large oil can, and he drank like an animal. This was an unusual case. When I arrived at the house, I paused at the front door and heard what sounded like a ferocious animal. Then, I saw that his body resembled that of an animal. It was terrible, and I felt very afraid. It was one of the first experiences I had in this region. I prayed and cast out the demons, and he became a Christian.

After a few years, he went to Sao Paulo. One day, I found him at a gas station. He had a Bible in his car and told me he was standing firm with the Lord. His wife shared that before his release, a pastor from another Church prayed with him, and the devil manifested himself and exposed the intercessor, revealing all the sins he was committing.

Shortly after, that church leader had to leave the city in the early morning because he had gotten a young woman from his church pregnant, causing a scandal in that small town. We must go where the Lord takes us. We do not have to be seeking to prove that we have the gift; if the Lord wants to use us, He Himself will lead us to do His work. We do not need to prove anything to anyone; we must be confident. We cannot listen to what people say, we must please only God.

In another case, I went to a house to pray for a woman who manifested demons. When I arrived at her house, she had decided to get rid of all her objects of idolatry. I never throw anything out of people's homes; I do not place my hands on what is not mine; I guide them and leave them free. That woman wanted to get rid of a picture of an image of idolatry. She threw it in the trash, but a layperson was asked to take the painting and said, in a playful tone, that pastors always ask to get rid of those objects. He took it to his house and placed it on the wall of his living room.

The woman told me that later, the man had to throw the painting far away from his home because his wife had begun to convulse at night. She did not stop convulsing until he got rid of the painting. It turns out that there were entities connected to that picture; there were covenants and alliances with demons. However, I do not get rid of people's things. I preach and teach the gospel of Jesus and pray. Then they themselves will decide what they will do. Obviously, when they ask about something, I share the truth with them.

Finally, I want to conclude by encouraging all who feel called to the ministry of deliverance to dedicate themselves fully and to trust that God Himself will provide opportunities for them to be used. Our role is merely to consecrate ourselves to the Lord's work.

I earnestly hope that these reflections and experiences help you develop your ministry in an increasingly effective way. I began this book by talking about my personal testimony of deliverance, and I have the honor to finish it, knowing that I could speak of many other experiences that the Lord has given me. Many have identified with my story, and I have also dealt with many other much worse cases. My greatest joy is knowing that through my life, I can demonstrate God's love for people in a practical way.

# Conclusion
# God's Perfect Plan

When I finished this book in 2010, I was sure that I would live in Quebec, Canada, to be an assistant pastor. Everything was organized for that. We had a rental house. My daughter was enrolled in school. But we were prevented by the Holy Spirit from going to Canada (Acts 16). They called me from the consulate and explained to me that because my daughter had certain disabilities, the government would not allow her a visa. They gave a visa to Shirley and me but not to her. So, at that moment, all our plans fell apart. I had left a very good church where we were very happy and could see a lot of growth.

At that time, we didn't have a house, church, salary, furniture, or car because we sold everything and donated some to the families. We were very frustrated, and I came to question my calling and all the signs that God had given me. But that year (2010) was when I was able to see many miracles from God. In that year I was able to visit more than 60 churches around Brazil in many cities and states, preaching and doing the ministry. So, I was able to see God's provision in many ways. Until April 2010 I was living at my mother-in-law's house, since the deadline to receive our daughter's visa was until April. But after her visa was denied, we had to go somewhere else to live.

The Church conference decided to help us with some monthly support, but that support was only to pay the rent for an apartment.

But since I didn't have any more furniture, I had to buy it. But I didn't have the money for that. We had spent a lot of money to have all the clinical examinations and documents to obtain a Canadian visa.

Then, one day, I was walking through the streets of Londrina, and I said, "God, I'm going to visit some real estate companies, and I need a miracle from you." I visited one, and I told the people who greeted me, "I'm here because I need a miracle."

They told me, "We don't do miracles here. We just rent and sell apartments and houses." But I told them that I needed an apartment with all the furniture for a year and based on the budget I had. The first company had nothing, but in the second, a miracle happened--an apartment with all furniture and utensils. The owner had put it up for rent for only one year and did not want to sell her furniture because she was thinking about moving back in after spending a year living with her father. (He had been through a very serious accident in which his wife had been killed.) So, I got that apartment in a very good place in the city.

God provided us with that place, and from that small but very complete apartment, we were able to live and, from there, visit many cities and churches to preach. We lived that year almost exclusively on spontaneous offers. It was during that time that I decided to write this book, but I did it as a very simple pamphlet to share my story with people and present and sell it in the churches where I preached. I did it, and the first time, I sold a thousand copies. Later I remembered that, in a pastors' course, someone

71

from a publishing house told us that if any of us had any writing to publish, we could contact her, and she would help.

I took her card, called her and told her about my book, sent her a copy, and they approved it. That year, in October, I launched this book at the national Christian book fair in Sao Paulo. To the glory of God, so far, I have sold almost 10 thousand copies of this book in its Portuguese version. So far, God is using this book to bless many people. I really felt very strongly when I wrote it that it would be distributed to many nations, which we will be able to achieve now.

Apart from this, in 2011, I was a missionary in Peru. I began to travel through Peru. Then, I was elected to a continental position in the Church, and I began to travel throughout Latin America. After four years in Peru, I moved to Panama, where I currently live. Here I have been able to found a missionary organization called Asa-Movement, and I have also founded and planted the Global Methodist Church of Panama. From Panama, I have traveled to more than 49 countries, preaching and sharing the Word of God. But I will tell the details of these recent stories in my next book, in which I will precisely emphasize the provision in God's plans.

May God bless you and use you

For His honor and glory!